1 Introduction

The decline in U.S. real GDP growth volatility after the early 1980s is well documented in the literature and it is coined as the Great Moderation by Stock and Watson (2003).[1] The causes of the Great Moderation mentioned in the literature mostly include: better monetary policy, better inventory management and good luck.

In this paper, I use U.S. data for 22 sectors for the period 1947-2010 and I argue that the aggregate growth volatility has declined because of shifts in the production activity across different sectors. By taking a take a portfolio approach, I distinguish between the effect of changes in the sectoral covariances and sectoral composition in the the decline in aggregate volatility. Representing the economy as a portfolio of n sectors, the GDP growth volatility is given by:

$$\sigma^2_{t,GDP} = \omega'_t \Sigma_t \omega_t \tag{1}$$

where ω_t is an $n \times 1$ vector of sectoral shares at time t, and Σ is the $n \times n$ covariance matrix of sectoral growth rates. Similarly, the GDP growth is the weighted average of the sectoral growth rates. As shown in equation (1), the two determinants of GDP growth volatility are the covariances of the sectoral growth rates and the sectoral allocations. A decline in the GDP growth volatility would be the outcome of a decrease in the sectoral growth volatility or correlation across sectors. Furthermore, a shifting away from the more volatile sectors or a higher diversification across sectors would also lead to a decline in volatility.

To determine the effect of covariance and sectoral allocations, I present the growth and volatility in the economy in an efficient frontier framework. The growth-volatility efficient frontier is determined by the sectoral growth and covariances. The frontier is plotted in the GDP (volatility, growth) space and every point on the frontier represents a portfolio of sectors. The sectoral allocations on the frontier and the corresponding aggregate growth and volatility represent the maximum level of efficiency that the economy can achieve. An increase in the sectoral covariances or a decrease in the sectoral growth rates will shift the frontier and shrink the growth-volatility opportunity set. I define the shifts in the frontier due to changes in the sectoral covariances, as changes in the risk opportunity set.

The location of the economy relative to the frontier is determined by the actual sectoral allocation. I define the optimal allocation as the one that minimizes the distance of the economy from the frontier, where the distance is measured in the (volatility, growth) space. I measure the efficiency of the economy as the distance between the economy and the optimal allocation on the frontier. The closer the economy to the frontier, the higher the efficiency. The distance along the volatility dimension represents risk efficiency.

Using this setup, I can distinguish between the two sources for the decline in GDP volatility: 1) decrease in covariances represented by an expansion of

---

[1] The decline in GDP growth volatility has been documented by Kim and Nelson (1999), McConnell and Perez-Quiros (2000) and Blanchard and Simon (2001).

the risk opportunity set and 2) changes in sectoral allocation represented by an increase in efficiency.

The set of 22 sectors used in this paper fully represents the U.S. economy. I use a one-sided 25-year rolling window to estimate the average sectoral growth rate and the sectoral covariances and to compute the frontier for each 25-year period between 1948 and 2010. I find that:

1. The frontier has shifted down and the growth volatility opportunity set has shrunk. At least 2/3 of the shrinkage is due to a lower sectoral growth, reflecting the productivity slowdown of the 1970s. The rest is due to a doubling of the growth volatility in Agriculture (1980), Information (1997) and Finance and Insurance (1998). There is no change in the growth volatility of the other sectors or in the correlation across sectors. This implies that the Great Moderation was not the outcome of a decline in sectoral covariances. As the GDP growth volatility is determined by the sectoral covariances and sectoral allocations, this suggests that the decline in GDP growth volatility was the outcome of changes in the sectoral allocations.

2. The distance of the economy from the frontier has decreased. The efficiency is estimated to have increased by 1.4 percentage points and it is interpreted as the decline in the growth volatility in the economy, if there were no changes in the sectoral covariances. This efficiency improvement is along the volatility dimension and is comparable to the 1.5 percentage points decline in GDP growth volatility in the data after the mid 1980s.

3. The economy became more diversified after the early 1980s. The economic activity has become more equally spread across sectors, shifting away from Agriculture and Manufacturing towards services. Notably, the share of Finance and Insurance has increased steadily from 2.4% of GDP in 1947 to 8.4% in 2010. It became the third largest sector in the last decade, which coupled with the doubling of the growth volatility in this sector, contributed to the recent increase in GDP growth volatility.

To conclude, as a result of changes in the sectoral allocation, the economy has moved closer to the growth-volatility frontier. The Great Moderation was the outcome of more risk efficient and more diversified sectoral allocations.

There is a growing literature on the Great Moderation. The conclusion in this paper is closely related to Carvalho and Gabaix (2010). They define fundamental volatility as a weighted average of the variance of the total factor productivity of each sector, where the sectoral variance is constant over time. They derive GDP growth volatility to be proportional to the fundamental volatility. They conclude that the changes in fundamental volatility, therefore changes in GDP volatility, would come only from changes in the sectoral composition, corresponding to a more diversified economy.

Sectoral diversification captures one dimension of the changes in the sectoral allocation. This paper further contributes to the literature by introducing a measure of the efficiency of the sectoral allocations. Given the sectoral covariances, this measure converts the complexity of the changes in sectoral allocations into changes in efficiency.

Other explanations of the Great Moderation include: better monetary policy (Clarida, Gali and Gertler 2000, Cecchetti, Flores-Lagues and Krause 2006), and better inventory management (Kahn, McConnell, and Perez-Quiros 2002, McCarthy and Zakrajšek 2007, Irvine and Schuh 2005). This paper looks at the aggregate output from the production approach using the value added by sector and the role of inventory management is not explicit.[2] However, the results in this paper do not reject the inventory hypothesis. They rather imply that the sectoral shift from manufacturing to services, especially finance, has decreased the contribution of a volatile inventory holding sector to aggregate volatility, hence lowering aggregate volatility.

Finally some have looked at the technology shocks. Galí and Gambetti (2009) show that the Great Moderation can be explained by the the change in the contribution of technology and non technology shocks. The findings in this paper do not explicitly exclude these factors, rather acknowledge that their impact might be channeled through the changes in the economic structure. Using counterfactual analysis, I show that the change in sectoral allocations is sufficient to explain the decline in GDP growth volatility. This paper weakens the case for the good luck hypothesis, as in smaller shocks, presented by Stock and Watson (2003).

In a broader perspective, this paper relates to the literature that uses sectoral data, an approach that has gained prominence in explaining cross-country differences in the level of production diversification and aggregate volatility. In cross-country studies, Imbs and Wacziarg (2003) find a U-shaped pattern of the sectoral diversification along different stages of development and Koren and Tenreyro (2007) find that sectoral diversification can explain the variation in aggregate volatility across countries.

This paper is organized as follows. Section 2 presents the sectoral allocation in a growth-volatility efficient frontier framework. Section 3 discusses the data. The results are presented in Section 4. Section 5 continues with some robustness checks and extensions and Section 6 concludes.

2 Sectoral Allocation in an Efficient Frontier Framework

In this section, I present a model of sectoral allocation in a growth-volatility efficient frontier framework. The efficient frontier is computed using the sectoral growth rates and sectoral covariances, and it provides the most risk efficient allocations that the economy can achieve. Given the sectoral growth rates and

---

[2]Value added by sector is defined as the difference between the sales and the value of intermediate inputs. The components of value added are: compensation of employees, taxes on production minus subsidies, and gross operating surplus.

covariances, the observed growth and volatility in the economy will be determined by the observed sectoral shares. The closer the economy is to this efficient frontier, the more risk efficient the economy is. This set up allows for the identification of the two sources of changes in GDP volatility: 1) changes in the covariances, represented by an expansion of the growth-volatility opportunity set, and 2) changes in sectoral allocation resulting in changes in efficiency.

Efficient frontier: Given the sectoral growth rates and covariances, what is the sectoral allocation that yields the lowest GDP growth variance for a given value of GDP growth? This set of sectoral allocations and the corresponding GDP growth and volatility represent the efficient frontier.

The inputs in the computation of the efficient frontier are the vector of the expected sectoral growth rates and the covariance matrix of the sectoral growth rates. At any time t, given the vector of sectoral growth rates g_t, the covariance matrix of the sectoral growth rates Σ_t and the vector of sectoral allocations ω_t, the GDP growth rate is given by:

$$g_{GDP,t} = \omega_t' g_t \qquad (2)$$

the expected GDP growth rate is given by:

$$E(g_{GDP,t}) = \omega_t' E_t(g) \qquad (3)$$

and the variance of the GDP growth rate is given by:

$$\sigma^2_{GDP,t} = \omega_t' \Sigma_t \omega_t \qquad (4)$$

where $\Sigma_t = E_t[(g_t - E_t(g))(g_t - E_t(g))']$ is an $n \times n$ covariance matrix of sectoral growth rates.

A sectoral allocation is efficient, if for a given GDP growth rate, μ, it yields the lowest GDP growth volatility. The efficient allocation, $\tilde{\omega}$, solves the following optimization problem:

$$\tilde{\omega} = argmin_\omega \{\omega' \Sigma \omega, \ s.t. \ (\omega' E(g) = \mu, \ \omega' 1 = 1, \ \omega \leq 1, \ \omega \geq 0)\} \qquad (5)$$

Repeating (5) for every possible value of GDP growth, I compute the efficient frontier as a set of efficient sectoral allocations, $\tilde{\omega}$, the corresponding GDP growth, $E(g_{GDP}) = \tilde{\omega}' E(g)$ and volatility, $\sigma^2_{GDP} = \tilde{\omega}' \Sigma \tilde{\omega}$.[3] The efficient frontier is plotted in the (volatility, growth) space. A higher sectoral growth rate, a lower sectoral variance or a smaller correlation across sectors will shift the efficient frontier, expanding the growth-volatility opportunity set. The shifts in the frontier, due to changes in the sectoral covariances, represent changes in the "risk opportunity".

Preferences: The economy likes GDP growth and dislikes GDP volatility.

Optimal allocation: Each of the sectoral allocations along the frontier is risk efficient. As the economy likes GDP growth and dislikes GDP volatility, the optimal risk efficient allocation is given by the portfolio on the frontier that

---

[3] The range of values for μ is determined by the range of the sectoral growth rates: $\mu = [min(g), max(g)]$.

is closest to the economy. The distance of the economy from the frontier is measured in the (volatility, growth) space.

The optimal sectoral allocation, $\tilde{\omega}_{optimal}$ at time t, is given by:

$$\tilde{\omega}_{optimal,t} = argmin_{\tilde{\omega}_i}\{D_t(\tilde{\omega}_i)\} \tag{6}$$

where $D_{i,t}(\tilde{\omega})$ denotes the distance of the economy from the sectoral allocation $\tilde{\omega}_i$.

I compute the distance of the economy from each of the sectoral allocations on the frontier as:

$$D_{i,t}(\tilde{\omega}) = [(g_{frontier,i,t} - g_{GDP,t})^2 + (\sigma_{frontier,i,t} - \sigma_{GDP,t})^2]^{1/2} \tag{7}$$

where, t is time, i indexes portfolios (sectoral allocations) on the efficient frontier, $D_{i,t}$ is the distance of the economy from the portfolio i on the frontier for time t. The growth rate and the variance for the ith portfolio on the frontier is given by $g_{frontier,i,t}$ and $\sigma_{frontier,i,t}$, respectively, which represent the GDP growth and variance if the sectoral allocations in the economy were the same as the sectoral allocations of the ith portfolio on the frontier. The observed GDP growth and volatility are denoted by $g_{GDP,t}$ and $\sigma_{GDP,t}$. Because the efficient frontier is concave and upward slopping, at $\tilde{\omega}_{optimal,t}$, the GDP growth will be no less than the observed GDP growth and the GDP volatility will be no higher than the observed GDP volatility.

The distance of the economy from the frontier, D, is the distance from the optimal allocation on the frontier, as in:

$$D_t = D(\tilde{\omega}_{optimal,t}) \tag{8}$$

Efficiency: I define the efficiency of the economy as the distance of the economy from the optimal allocation, as in equation (8), where the distance is measured in the (growth, volatility) space. I define the risk efficiency as the distance attributed to the volatility dimension. In this efficient frontier framework of sectoral allocation, the two sources for a change in GDP volatility, changes in the sectoral covariances and sectoral allocations, are converted into changes in the risk opportunity set, and changes in the risk efficiency of the economy.

3 Data

The sectoral data is available from the Bureau for Economic Analysis. The data is available at an annual frequency, for the period 1947-2010 for 22 broad sectors of the economy. The list of sectors is given in Table 1 and they fully represent the economy. These sectors correspond to the 2-digit level of the 2002 North American Industry Classification System (NAICS). The sectoral data for the period 1947-1987 is available only at the 2 digit level. The more disaggregated data (at a 3-digit level) is available starting from 1987. The data includes two variables: chain-type quantity index for value added (*vaqi*) and value added as a percentage of GDP (*vapct*). The sectoral growth rate is given by $g_{i,t} = \Delta \log(vaqi_{i,t})$. Let $\omega_{i,t} \equiv vapct_{i,t}$, then $\sum \omega_i = 1$, $g_{GDP} \equiv \omega' g$, and $\sigma_{GDP}^2 \equiv \omega' \Sigma \omega$. Whelan (2000) shows that in the case of chain-type indices, g_{GDP} as given in the National Income and Product Account (NIPA), would satisfy ($g_{GDP} \equiv \omega' g$), if ($\omega' g$) represented contributions. As *vapct* is defined as a nominal share, its product with the sectoral growth rate represents growth contributions. As shown in Figure 1, the GDP growth rate series from the NIPA and the GDP growth series using the sectors' growth rate and nominal shares match.

The existence, timing and magnitude of the Great Moderation using annual data. There is consensus in the literature on the start date of the Great Moderation as the first quarter of 1984. This break date is estimated using quarterly data for GDP growth. Since the sectoral data is available at an annual frequency, I test for the existence and the timing of the break in the GDP growth volatility using annual data. Following McConnell and Perez-Quiros (2000), and Stock and Watson (2002), I compute the instantaneous volatility as,

$$\sigma_t = \sqrt{\frac{\pi}{2}} |\epsilon_t| \qquad (9)$$

where ϵ_t is the estimated error term from the following AR(1) model of real GDP growth rates: $\Delta y_t = \alpha + \beta \Delta y_{t-1} + \epsilon_t$, where y_t is the log of real GDP. Figure 2 plots the HP trend of the instantaneous volatility.

I test the null hypothesis of no breaks, $\gamma_1 = 0$, against the alternative of a single break, in the following regression:

$$\sigma_t = \gamma_0 + \gamma_1 D_t + \xi_t \qquad (10)$$

where D_t is a dummy variable assuming a value of 1 for time $t \geq \tau$, given an estimated break date $\tau \in [T_1, T_2]$, where T_1 and T_2 are defined using 15% trimming.[4] Using Bai and Perron's (1998) Sup-F statistics and Perron and Qu (2006), I find support for a break in the GDP volatility.[5] The estimated break date is 1984. The estimated values for GDP volatility before and after 1984 are 2.9 and 1.4 respectively, which imply a halving of the GDP volatility after 1984. These results confirm 1984 as the estimated break date in the GDP growth volatility and confirm the estimated magnitude of the decline in GDP volatility.

Variance decomposition. As an initial diagnosis, Table 2 shows the variance decomposition of the GDP growth rate. The decomposition is based on the contribution of the sector's growth to GDP growth, which is defined as the product of the sectoral growth rate with the sectoral share ($\omega_i g_i$). By definition, the GDP growth volatility is the sum of the variance terms and the covariance terms of these contributions.

---

[4] In the case of a 15% trimming, $T_1 = 0.15N$ and $T_1 = 0.85N$, where N is the total number of observations.

[5] Following Perron and Qu (2006), I compute the Sup-F statistics, the critical value and the estimated break date. The Sup-F statistics is 12.614 and the 5% critical value is 8.592. I thank Perron and Qu for sharing their code. The code is available at http://people.bu.edu/perron/code.html.

The variance decomposition of the contributions shows that the decline in the sum of the variance and covariance terms is comparable to the decline in the variance of the GDP growth rate. Similar to Irvine and Schuh (2005), the decline in the covariance of the contributions accounts for about 70 % of the decline of the aggregate volatility. Carvalho and Gabaix (2010) show that because of input linkages, there is comovement across sectors. The changes in the off-diagonal terms in the covariance matrix would simply reflect changes in their measure of fundamental volatility, which is defined as the weighted average of the sectoral volatilities. They also show that, while all the shocks in their model are idiosyncratic, even small measurement errors can create comovement in total factor productivity.

4 Results

I use a one-sided 25-year rolling window to compute the frontier for each 25-year period between 1948 and 2010, where the first period starts in 1948 and the last periods ends in 2010. Figure 3 plots the efficient frontier for each 25-year period between 1948 and 2010. The first frontier is constructed for 1972 and it uses data on the sectoral growth rate for the period 1948-1972. The last frontier, the frontier for 2010, is constructed using data for the period 1986-2010. The color of the plots changes gradually, from dark blue to light green, where the dark blue corresponds to the earlier periods and the light green to the later ones.

I observe that:

1. *The efficient frontier has shifted down.* This implies that over the period 1948-2010, if there were no changes in the sectoral allocation, the GDP volatility would have increased and the GDP growth would have decreased. Most of the shifts are along the growth dimension, suggesting that the shifts should be mainly due to a lower sectoral growth rate. The curvature of the frontiers is relatively unchanged, implying that there is no change in the correlation across sectors.

2. *The distance of the economy from the frontier has decreased.* The decline in the sectoral growth rates, captured by the growth dimension of the shifts in the frontier, is higher than decline in the GDP growth in the data. Also the decline in the distance is mostly along the volatility dimension. That is, the economy became more risk efficient.

These observations are elaborated in the following subsections.

4.1 Efficient Frontier and Growth-Volatility Opportunity Set

To get a time series of the shifting down of the frontier, I compute the distance of the each frontier from the first frontier. The distance is measured in the (volatility, growth) space. Note that each frontier is computed by constructing

N portfolios which are equally spaced in the range of the growth rates for that frontier. For each frontier, I calculate the distance between the corresponding i portfolios, where $i = 1$ to N, as:

$$D_{t,i,1} = [(g_{frontier,i,t} - g_{frontier,i,1})^2 + (\sigma_{frontier,i,t} - \sigma_{frontier,i,1})^2]^{1/2} \quad (11)$$

The distance of each frontier from the first one is given by the average distance between the corresponding portfolios as in equation (12).

$$D_{t,1} = mean_i\{D_{t,i,1}\} \quad (12)$$

Figure 4 plots the distance of each frontier from the first frontier.

The distance is interpreted as the expected increase in GDP volatility or the expected decline in GDP growth in that period relative to the first one. For example, when comparing the last frontier (period 1986-2010) with the first one (period 1948-1972), a distance of 2.418 can be interpreted as: if there were no change in the efficiency of the economy, the growth GDP volatility would be up to 2.418 percentage points higher or the average growth rate would be up to 2.418 percentage points lower.

The shifting down of the frontier can be the outcome of a higher sectoral variance, a lower correlation across sectors or a lower sectoral growth. I compute the contribution of the changes in sectoral growth, volatility and correlation, by computing counterfactual frontiers where I allow for only one of these three variables to change. To distinguish between the effect of a change in the sectoral growth and sectoral covariance, I compute a counterfactual frontier, using the sectoral growth from the first period, 1948-1972, and the covariance matrix from the period (1948+n) to (1948+n+25), where n takes values from 1 to 38. For example the counterfactual frontier for the last period, 1986-2010, is computed using the vector of sectoral growth rate from the period 1948-1972 and the covariance matrix from the period 1986-2010.

I further decompose the change in the covariance matrix into a change in the sectoral variance and correlation across sectors. I compute a counterfactual covariance matrix as

$$\sigma^{2,n}_{i,j,counterfactual} = \rho^{(1948+n)to(1948+n+25)}_{i,j} \sigma^{1948-1972}_i \sigma^{1948-1972}_j \quad (13)$$

where, $n = 1, 2, ...38$, i and j denoted sectors and the superscripts denote the corresponding periods. For example the counterfactual frontier for the last period, 1986-2010, is computed using the vector of sectoral growth rate from the period 1948-1972 and the covariance matrix as

$$\sigma^{2,1986-2010}_{i,j,counterfactual} = \rho^{1986-2010}_{i,j} \sigma^{1948-1972}_i \sigma^{1948-1972}_j \quad (14)$$

Figure 5 plots a time series decomposition of the frontier shifts due to changes in the sectoral growth rate, variance and correlation. The vertical axis measures the distance of each frontier from the first frontier. A non - zero slope represents a shift in the frontier for the corresponding period. For example, the frontiers computed using data until the mid 80s, have shifted due to changes in the sectoral growth rates, variances and correlation. During this period, while the growth effect is larger, the magnitude of the shifts is comparable across the three factors. However, the variance and the correlation effect for the latter frontiers is either unchanged or smaller, as the variance effect (the red line) is almost flat and the correlation effect (the blue line) is flat and slightly downward sloping in the latest period. The illustration of the decomposition of these effects for the latest frontier is shown in Figure 6. The latest frontier is computed using the data for the period 1986-2010 and as such it almost fully represents the period of the Great Moderation. It is evident that the frontier has shifted down because of a lower sectoral growth rate, and a higher sectoral variance. A lower sectoral growth accounts for 2/3 of the shift in the frontier, representing the productivity slowdown in the 1970s.[6]

I test for breaks in growth volatility for each of the sectors. The Sup-F statistics, estimated break date and volatilities are given in Table 3. I find support for no change in the sectoral volatility for 19 sectors and an increase in sectoral volatility in 3 sectors: Agriculture, Information and Finance and Insurance. Figure 7 plots the sectoral volatility for these three sectors. As the sectoral variance has been higher and there has been no change in the correlation across sectors, we expect to observe a higher GDP volatility. Instead, the GDP volatility has decreased, implying that the decline in the GDP volatility was due to changes in the sectoral allocations.

4.2 Efficiency

Figure 3 suggested that the economy has been getting closer to the frontier. I defined the efficiency of the economy as the distance of the economy from the frontier. Figure 8 shows that the distance of the economy from the frontier has been decreasing over time, i.e. the economy has become more efficient. The distance of the economy from the frontier was 2.32 in the period 1948-1972 and 0.93 in the period 1986-2010. The change in the efficiency of the economy from the period 1948-1972 to the period 1986-2010, given by the difference in distances, equals 1.39. Interpreted in terms of volatility, this implies that, if there were no change in the covariance matrix, the GDP growth volatility in the period 1986-2010 would be 1.39 percentage points lower than in the period 1948-1972. This improvement in efficiency is comparable to the 1.5 percentage points decline in the GDP growth volatility after 1984. To illustrate the effect of the increased efficiency of the economy in the decline of GDP volatility, I compute the counterfactual values for growth and volatility in the period 1986-2010, if there were no changes in the efficiency of the economy.

I set the efficiency at the period 1948-1972. In the (volatility, growth) space, I use the vector between the optimal portfolio and the economy in the period 1986-2010 and the distance of the economy from the frontier in the period 1948-1972 to locate the economy under this "what if" scenario. The results

---

[6]The shift due to the change in the average sectoral growth rate is 2.2126 and the shift due to the change in the covariance matrix is 0.9686.

are plotted in Figure 9. If there were no change in the efficiency, the GDP volatility in the period 1986-2010, would be 2.82%, which is almost the same as the GDP volatility in the data during the period 1948-1972. The distance of the economy from the frontier has two dimentions: growth and volatility. As such, the increased efficiency can be attributed to a decrease in the distance along the growth or the volatility dimension.

A decrease in the distance along the growth (volatility) dimension implies a decline in the difference between the growth (volatility) observed in the data and the growth (volatility) at the optimal allocation. Figure 10 plots the growth rate and volatility at the optimal sectoral allocation, the GDP growth and volatility observed in the data, and the difference between the two. Figure 10 shows that the difference between the growth volatility in the data and the volatility at the optimal allocation has been decreasing over time. The increase in the efficiency occured along the volatility dimension, an increase in risk efficiency.

4.3 Sectoral Allocation

In the previous section, I showed that since the sectoral covariances have either increased or not changes, the Great Moderation was the outcome of changes in the sectoral allocations. Furthermore, the risk efficiency, as measured by the difference between the GDP volatility in the data vs.the model, has increased. These findings imply that the sectoral allocations were more risk efficient. From Finance, a lower volatility can be a benefit of diversification. To illustrate, I present a measure of sectoral diversification, which refers to the dispersion of the economic activity across sectors.

Figure 11 plots, the Herfindal Index, the most commonly used index of sectoral concentration.[7] The Herfindal Index, (HI), is defined as,

$$HI_t = \sum \omega_{i,t}^2 \tag{15}$$

where $\omega_{i,t}$ is the sector share to GDP, denoted by the variable *vapct* in the data. A decrease in the Herfindal index corresponds to an increase in diversification, implying that the economic activity is more equally spread across sectors. The U.S. economy was more diversified during the Great Moderation. Figure 12 shows that there is a decline in the sector share for the Manufacturing of Durable and Nondurables goods, and Agriculture and an increase in services, particularly Finance and Insurance, Health, Professional and Administration services. As shown in Table 3, the growth volatility in Finance and Insurance and Information doubled after 1998/1999, contributing to the increase in the volatility in the recent years.

Figure 11 suggests that there are two breaks (three regimes) in the HI series. I find strong evidence for the presence of two breaks.[8] The estimated break

---

[7] Other measures of sectoral concentration, such as the Coefficient of Variation and the Max-Min spread of sectoral shares show the same pattern. The correlation (HI, coefficient of variation) is 0.9997 and the correlation(HI, Max-Min spread) is 0.945.

[8] The Sup-F statistics is 129.229 and the 1% critical value is 9.801.

dates are the 1970 and 1980, where the period 1970-1980 corresponds to the decline in the sectoral concentration and the period 1980 onwards corresponds to the period of a higher sectoral diversification. While the estimated date for the second break in the HI, 1980, occurs before the estimated break date in the GDP volatility, 1984, the 90% confidence interval for the second break in HI falls within the 90% confidence interval for a break in the GDP growth volatility.[9]

To further illustrate the effect of changes in the sectoral allocation in the decline of GDP growth volatility, I construct a counterfactual GDP growth series, using the sectoral growth rates in the data and setting the sectoral composition as in 1948:

$$g_{GDP,t,counterfactual} = \sum g_{i,t}\omega_{i,1948} \tag{16}$$

I compute the instantaneous volatility of $g_{GDP,t,counterfactual}$. Figure 13 plots the GDP volatility in the data and the GDP volatility for the counterfactual growth series.

The only difference between these two series comes from the changes in the sectoral allocations over time. Figure 13 shows that the effect of the changes in the sectoral allocation occurs in the mid 1980s. I cannot reject the hypothesis of no break in the counterfactual GDP growth series. The change in sectoral allocations is sufficient to explain the decline in GDP growth volatility.

5 Robustness Checks and Extensions

5.1 Robustness Checks

In this section, I test for the robustness of results using a less disaggregated classification and a more rigid frontier, where the sectoral shares are allowed to move within certain bounds.

Sectoral Classification. The selection of the 22 sectors, corresponding to the 2-digit NAICS, was dictated by the data availability. To test the robustness of the results with respect to the sectoral classification, I use 15 sectors corresponding to the sector level classification in the Input-Output Tables. The list of sectors is given in Table 4. I cannot test the robustness of the results for a less disaggregated classification as the data at a 3-digit level data is availabe starting from 1987, leaving out the period before the Great Moderation.

Bounds on Sectoral Shares. When computing the efficient frontier, the sectoral shares were just constrained to be between 0 and 1 and to sum up to 1, allowing for a very feasible structure of the economy. To introduce rigidities, I impose further constraints on the sectoral shares. I set the lower (L) and the upper bounds (U) as:

$$\omega_{L,i} = max\{0, [min(vapct_i) - 3stdev(vapct_i)]\} \tag{17}$$

$$\omega_{U,i} = min\{1, [max(vapct_i) + 3stdev(vapct_i)]\} \tag{18}$$

---

[9]The 90% confidence interval: $GDPvolatility = [1974, 1996]$. $HI = [1979, 1987]$.

Furthermore, I define 15 groups as in the sector level classification of the Input-Output Table. I impose bounds on the relative share of groups as follows:

$$\left(\frac{\omega_{group_i}}{\omega_{group_j}}\right)_L = max\left\{0, \left[min\left(\frac{vapct_{group_i}}{vapct_{group_j}}\right) - 3stdev\left(\frac{vapct_{group_i}}{vapct_{group_j}}\right)\right]\right\} \quad (19)$$

$$\left(\frac{\omega_{group_i}}{\omega_{group_j}}\right)_U = max\left(\frac{vapct_{group_i}}{vapct_{group_j}}\right) + 3stdev\left(\frac{vapct_{group_i}}{vapct_{group_j}}\right) \quad (20)$$

The allocations along the efficient frontier are computed as in equation 21.

$$\tilde{\omega} = argmin_\omega\{\omega'\Sigma\omega, \ s.t. \ (\omega'E(g) = \mu, \omega'1 = 1, \ \omega \leq 1,$$
$$\omega_L \leq \omega \leq \omega_U$$
$$\left(\frac{\omega_{group_i}}{\omega_{group_j}}\right)_L \leq \left(\frac{\omega_{group_i}}{\omega_{group_j}}\right) \leq \left(\frac{\omega_{group_i}}{\omega_{group_j}}\right)_U)\} \quad (21)$$

Table 5 shows the correlation coefficient for the measures of frontier shifts, efficiency and risk efficiency produced by these two specifications with the 22-sector baseline. I find that the results are robust to the less disaggregated classification and robust to the constraints on the sectoral shares: the growth-volatility opportunity set has shrunk, the economy has become more efficient and the improvement in efficiency is along the volatility dimension.

Table 6 shows the counterfactual GDP volatility for the period 1986-2010 if there were no changes in efficiency. The GDP volatility for the period 1948-1972 was 2.62 %. If the efficiency in 1986-2010 were the same as in the 1948-1972, the counterfactual GDP volatility produced by the 22-sector, 15-sector and 22-sector with sectoral share bounds would be 2.41%, 2.64% and 2.82% respectively. These results confirm that the decline the GDP volatility was the outcome of more risk efficient sectoral allocations.

The Herfindal Index, both in the 22-sector and 15-sector case, shows an increase in sectoral diversification, implying that the more diversified sectoral allocations were more risk efficient.[10]

5.2 Extensions

Preferences. The frontier is determined by the vector of the sectoral growth rate and the covariance matrix of the sectoral growth rates. Given the frontier, the actual sectoral allocations determine the location of the economy relative to the frontier. The preferences in terms of growth and volatility are represented in the distance of the economy from the frontier as in equation (7). The optimal allocation then corresponds to efficient allocation that minimizes the distance of the economy from the frontier in the (growth, volatility) space. I use the ratio of growth-to-volatility at the optimal allocation to capture the "revealed" preferences. Figure 14 plots the ratio of growth-to-volatility in the data and the

---

[10]The correlation coefficient for the Herfindal Index in the 22-sector and 15-sector classification is 0.986.

optimal allocation on the frontier computed for three specifications: 22-sector and 15-sector classsification and the 22-sector with bounds on sectoral shares.

The growth-to-volatility ratio in the economy is stable at about 2. Across the three specifications, the growth-to-volatility ratio of the optimal allocation is higher and volatile in the period before the Great Moderation. During the Great Moderation, the ratio is in the range of 2 to 4, which is also the range usually used for the coefficient of risk aversion in the the mean-variance utility function.

Sectoral Volatility and Trade Balance. While the trade volume has been increasing since the 1950s, the Great Moderation corresponds to a period of persistent trade deficits, as plotted in Figure 15. Figure 16 plots the trade balance and growth volatility for each sector. Figure 16 shows that the sectors with a trade deficit (Durables, Mining and Non durables) are among the more volatile sectors.

This suggests another point of view of the Great Moderation, as an outcome of "exporting volatility" by incurring a trade deficit in the more volatile sectors. It is not plausible to suggest that the increased trade openness led to an increase in growth volatility in these sectors, as I did not find support for a change in volatility in these sectors.

6 Concluding Remarks

Modeling the economy in the (growth, volatility) space, I can present the sectoral allocation in a growth-volatility efficient frontier and discuss the contribution of changes in sectoral covariances and sectoral allocations in explaining the Great Moderation. I convert the complexity of changes in the sectoral allocations into a measure of efficiency of the economy. I measure the efficiency as the distance of the economy from the growth-volatility efficient frontier. While the frontier has shifted down, shrinking the growth-volatility opportunity set, the efficiency has increased.

I conclude that the decline in GDP growth volatility after 1984, up until the last recession, can be sufficiently explained by more efficient and more diversified sectoral allocations.

In addition, sectoral shifts have been proposed as an explanation for the slow increase in employement during the recoveries since the early 1990s. Risssman (2009) shows the structural changes were more prounounced in Finance, Insurance and Real Estate sector. These structural changes would contribute to the increase in the growth volatility in Finance and Insurance, which combined with the increase in the share of these sectors contributed to the recent increase in aggregate growth volatility.

Furthermore, the Great Moderation also concurs with a period of persistent trade deficits. These deficits were in the more volatile sectors. These facts suggest that the impact of the globalization on growth volatility is affected by the sectoral composition of the trade balance.

References

[1] Bai, Jushan, and Pierre Perron. 1998. Estimating and testing linear models with multiple structural changes. Econometrica 66(1), 47-78.

[2] Blanchard, Olivier, and John Simon. 2001. The long and large decline in U.S. output volatility. Brookings Papers on Economic Activity 2001(1), 165-71.

[3] Cavallo, Eduardo. 2007. Openness to trade and output volatility: a reassessment. Inter-American Development Bank Working Paper 604.

[4] Carvalho, Vasco M., and Xavier Gabaix. 2010. The great diversification and its undoing. National Bureau for Economic Research Working Paper16424.

[5] Cecchetti, Stephen G., Alfonso Flores-Lagunes, and Stefan Krause. 2006. Has monetary policy become more efficient? A cross-country analysis. The Economic Journal 116: 408-433.

[6] Clarida, Richard, Jordi Galí, and Mark Getler. 2000. Monetary policy rules and macroeconomic stability: evidence and some theory. Quarterly Journal of Economics 115(1), 147-180.

[7] Galí, Jordi and Luca Gambetti. 2009. On the sources of the great moderation. American Economic Journal: Macroeconomics 1(1), 26-57.

[8] Imbs, Jean. 2007. Growth and volatility. Journal of Monetary Economics 54, 1848-1862.

[9] Imbs, Jean and Romain Wacziarg. 2003. Stages of diversification. American Economic Review 93(1), 63-86.

[10] Irvine, Owen and Scott Schuh. 2005. The Roles of comovement and inventory investment in the reduction of output volatility. Federal Reserve Bank of Boston 05(9).

[11] Kahn, James, Margaret M. McConnell, and Gabriel Perez-Quiros. 2002. On the causes of the increased stability of the U.S. economy. Federal Reserve Bank of New York Economic Policy Review 8(1), 183 - 202.

[12] Kim, Chang-Jin, and Charles R. Nelson. 1999. Has the U.S. economy become more stable? A Bayesian approach based on a Markov-switching model of the business cycle. The Review of Economics and Statistics 81(4), 608-616.

[13] Koren, Miklós and Silvana Tenreyro. 2007. Volatility and development. Quarterly Journal of Economics, 122(1), 243-87.

[14] McCarthy, Jonathan and Egon Zakrajšek. 2007. Inventory dynamics and business cycles: What has changed? Journal of Money, Credit, and Banking 39(2-3), 591-613.

[15] McConnell, Margaret and Gabriel Perez-Quiros. 2000. Output fluctuations in the United States: What has changed since the early 1980's. American Economic Review 90(5), 1464-76.

[16] Perron, Pierre and Zhongjun Qu. 2006. Estimating restricted structural change models. Journal of Econometrics 134(2), 373-399.

[17] Rissman, Ellen R. 2009. Employment growth: cyclical movements or structural change? Federal Reserve Bank of Chicago Economic Perspectives 33(4), 44-57.

[18] Stock, James and Mark Watson. 2003. Has the business cycle changed? Evidence and explanations. FRB Kansas City symposium, Jackson Hole, Wyoming, August 28-30, 2003.

[19] Whelan, Karl. 2000. A guide to the use of chain aggregated NIPA data. Board of Governors of the Federal Reserve System Working Paper 2000(35).

Abbreviation	Sector	2002 NAICS Code
Agri	Agriculture, Forestry, Fishing and Hunting	11
Mining	Mining	21
Utilities	Utilities	22
Construction	Construction	23
Durables	Durable goods	33, 321, 327
Nondurables	Nondurable goods	31, 32 (except 321&327)
Wholesale	Wholesale trade	42
Retail	Retail trade	44, 45
Transp	Transportation and Warehousing	48, 49 (except 491)
Info	Information	51
FinIns	Finance and Insurance	52
Real	Real estate, Rental, Leasing	53
ProfScien	Professional, Scientific and Technical Services	54
Manage	Management of Companies and Enterprises	55
Admin	Administrative and Waste Management Services	56
Education	Education services	61
Health	Health care and Social assistance	62
ArtsEntRec	Arts, Entertainment and Recreation	71
AccomFood	Accomodation and Food services	72
Other	Other Services, except Government	81
Fed	Federal Government	na
StateLocal	State and Local Government	na

Table 1: **List of Sectors.** The selection of the sectors is dictated by the data availability, as to include observations before and after the Great Moderation. The data for the period 1947-1987 is available only at the 2-digit level, representing 22 sectors. The more disaggregated data is available only starting from 1987. I do a robustness test using the sector-level classification of the Input-Output table, representing 15 sectors, and I find that the results are robust to a less disaggregated data.

	Early (1948-1983)	Late (1984-2010)	Late/Early
Variance Real GDP growth	7.32	3.07	0.42
Sum of the variance terms	2.05	0.77	0.38
Sum of the covariance terms	5.27	2.30	0.44

Table 2: **Variance Decomposition.** Sector's contribution to GDP growth is defined as the sector's growth rate weighted by the sector's share to GDP ($\omega_i g_i$). The sum of the variance terms is ($\sum \omega_i^2 \sigma_i^2$) and the sum of the covariance terms is ($2 \sum \omega_i \omega_j \rho_{i,j} \sigma_i \sigma_j$).

Sector	Sup-F	Date	Before	After
Agriculture, Forestry, Fishing and Hunting	8.934**	1980	3.8	9.5
Mining	6.341			
Utilities	4.279			
Construction	2.885			
Durable goods	4.555			
Nondurable goods	2.395			
Wholesale trade	3.579			
Retail trade	1.57			
Transportation and Warehousing	6.327			
Information	9.056**	1997	2.4	5.4
Finance and Insurance	13.785***	1998	2.5	5.3
Real estate, Rental, Leasing	3.662			
Professional, Scientific and Technical Services	1.87			
Management of Companies and Enterprises	5.178			
Administrative and Waste Management Services	4.178			
Education services	2.24			
Health care and Social assistance	5.759			
Arts, Entertainment and Recreation	6.984			
Accomodation and Food services	1.984			
Other Services, except Government	2.36			
Federal Government	2.043			
State and Local Government	4.004			

Table 3: **Breaks in Sectoral Volatility.** I find support for no change in the sectoral volatility for 19 sectors and an increase in sectoral volatility in 3 sectors: Agriculture, Information and Finance and Insurance. For these three sectors, Date, Before and After show the estimated break date, and the estimated volatility before and after the break date. The volatility in these three sectors has doubled. These results show that the decline in GDP growth volatility could have not been the outcome of a lower sectoral variance. Levels of significance: 1% (***), 5% (**).

Sector	I-O Codes	2002 NAICS codes
Agriculture, forestry, fishing, and hunting	11	11
Mining	21	21
Utilities	22	22
Construction	23	23
Manufacturing	31G	31, 32, 33
Wholesale trade	42	42
Retail trade	44RT	44, 45
Transportation and warehousing	48TW	48, 49 (except 491)
Information	51	51
Finance, insurance, real estate, rental, and leasing	FIRE	52, 53
Professional and business services	PROF	54, 55, 56
Educational services, health care, and social assistance	6	6
Arts, entertainment, recreation, accommodation, and food services	7	7
Other services, except government	81	81
Government	G	NA

Table 4: **Sector level Classification in the Input-Output Tables.** The sector-level classification of the Input-Output Tables corresponds to 15 sectors. The results are robust to this level of aggregation. The 3-digit data is available starting from 1987.

Correlation coefficient for	Frontier Shifts	Efficiency	Risk Efficiency
	22 sectors	22 sectors	22 sectors
22 sectors	1	1	1
15 sectors	0.979	0.995	0.994
22 sectors & sectoral shares bounds	0.965	0.974	0.866

Table 5: **Comparison of Different Specifications.** "Frontier shifts" measures the distance of each frontier from the first one. "Efficiency" is measured by the distance of the economy from the efficient allocation, and "Risk Efficiency" corresponds to the volatility dimension of "Efficiency". I test the robustness of the results to the level of dissagregation ("22 sectors" versus "15 sectors") and variability of sectoral shares ("22 sectors" versus "22 sectors & bounds"). In "22 sectors & bounds", the sector shares and the ratio of sector shares are bounded to $[min - 3stdev, max + 3stdev]$ of the observed values. The results are robust to these changes. The growth-volatility opportunities set has been shrinking and the risk efficiency has been increasing.

	GDP growth volatility
data (1948-1972)	2.62
data (1986-2010)	1.68
counterfactual (1986-2010) if efficiency as in (1948-2010)	
—22 sectors	2.41
—15 sectors	2.64
—22 sectors & sectoral shares bounds	2.82

Table 6: **GDP volatility and Efficiency.** The counterfactual GDP growth volatility is computed keeping the efficiency as in (1948-1972). Efficiency is measured by the distance of the economy from the frontier. The counterfactual GDP growth volatility in the three specifications is almost the same as the volatility in the data in (1948-1972), reconfirming that the decline in GDP volatility was the outcome of more risk efficient sectoral allocations. "22 sectors" is the baseline, "15 sectors" corresponds to a more aggregated datatset and "22 sectors & bounds" restricts the variability of the sector shares and the ratio of sector shares to $[min - 3stdev, max + 3stdev]$.

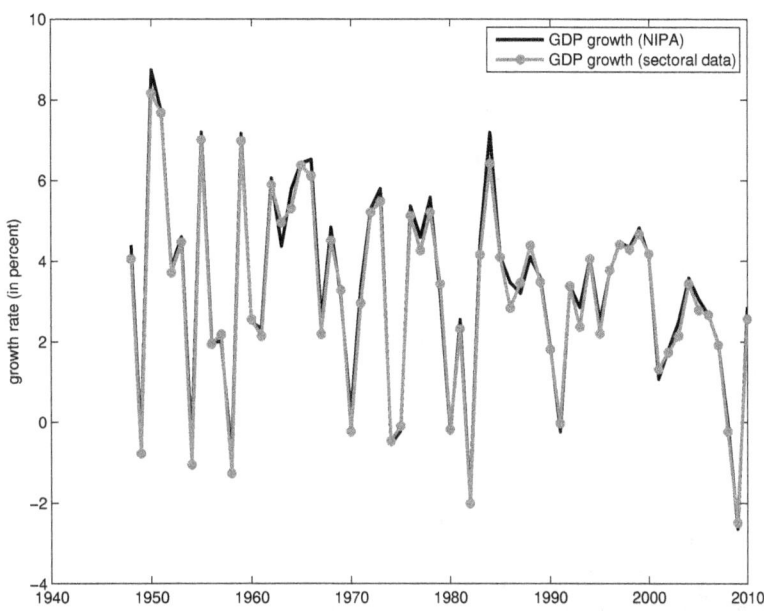

Figure 1: **The GDP growth rate from National Income and Product Accounts and as a weighted sum of the sectoral growth rates.**

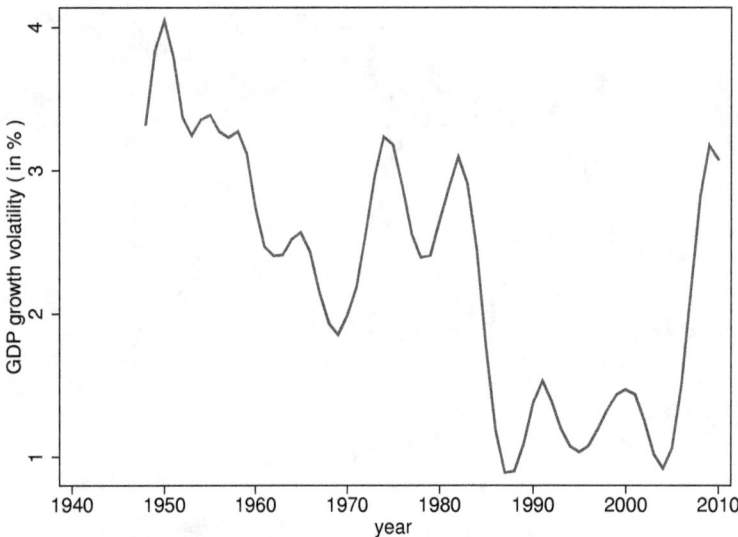

Figure 2: **HP Trend of Instantaneous GDP Growth Volatility.** The instantaneous GDP volatility is defined as $\sigma_t = \sqrt{\frac{\pi}{2}}\,|\epsilon_t|$, where ϵ_t is the error term from the AR(1) model of GDP growth. In the literature, the estimated start date of the decline in the GDP growth volatility is 1984:1. The estimated break date, using annual data, is 1984.

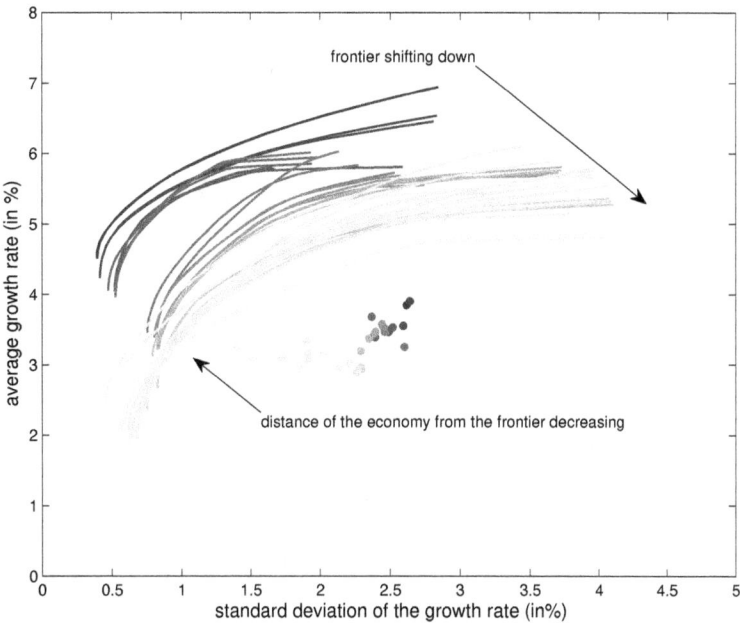

Figure 3: **The Efficient Frontier and the Economy Over Time.** Each line shows the efficient frontier for every 25-year rolling period between 1948 and 2010. The circles show the GDP growth and volatility observed in the data for every 25-year rolling period. There are 39 lines and 39 circles in this Figure. The distance of the economy from the frontier corresponds to distance of the circle from the line with the same color. The fontier has been shifting down to the right, implying that the opportunity set has shrunk. The distance of the economy from the frontier has decreased, implying that the efficiency of the economy has increased.

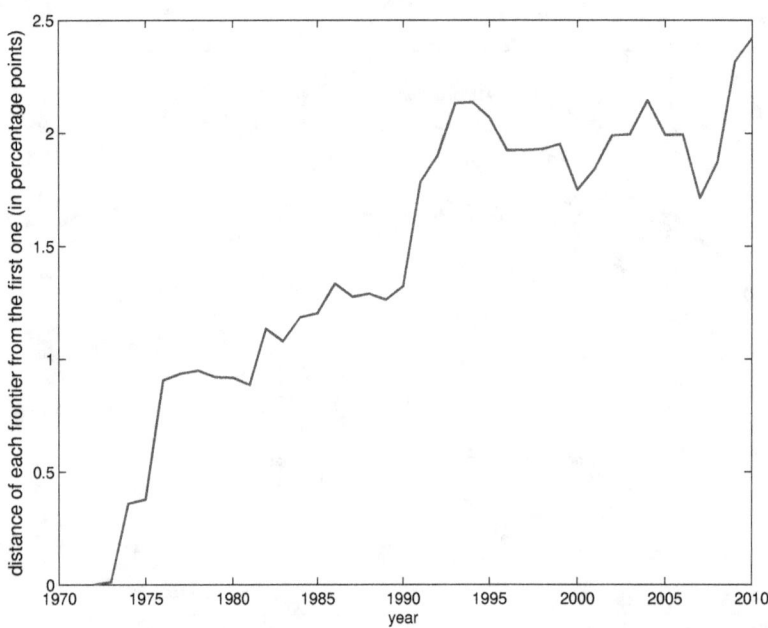

Figure 4: **Distance of each Frontier from the First Frontier.** The distance is interpreted as the expected increase in GDP volatility or the expected decline in GDP growth in the corresponding period relative to the first one, if there were no change in efficiency. For example, the distance of the last frontier (1986-2010) from the first frontier (1948-1872) is 2.418. If there were no change in the distance of the economy from the frontier, i.e. no change in the efficiency, the GDP growth volatility in the last period would be up to 2.418 percentage point higher than in the first period.

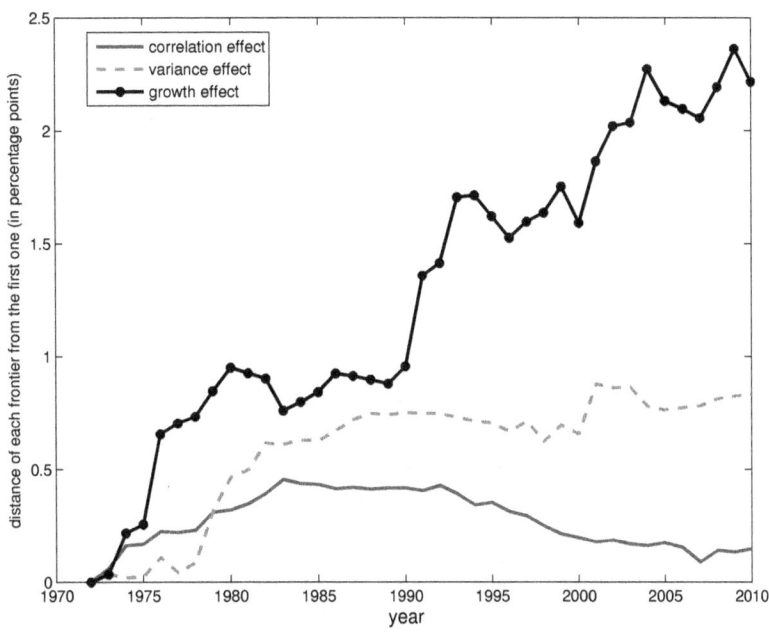

Figure 5: **Time Series of the Effect of Sectoral Growth, Variance and Correlation in Shifting the Frontier.** The vertical axis measures the distance of each frontier from the first frontier. A non - zero slope represents a shift in the frontier for the corresponding period.

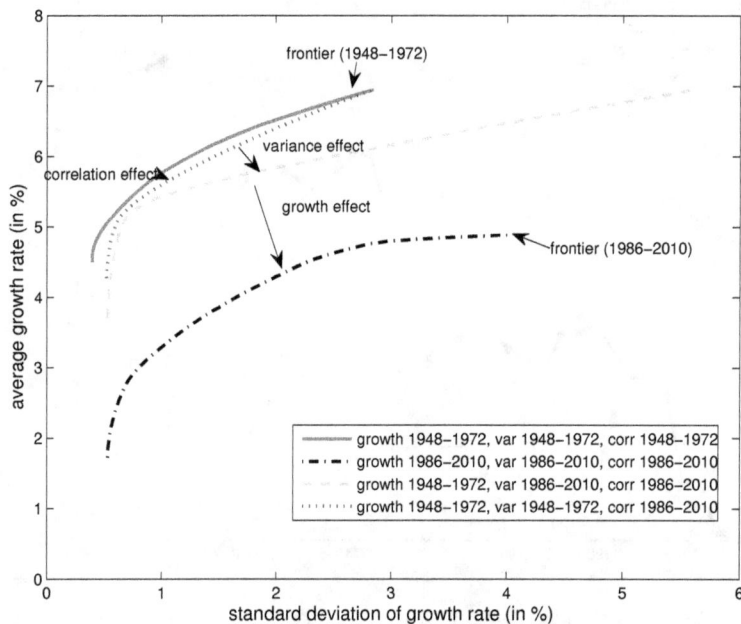

Figure 6: **Decomposing the Effect of Sectoral Growth, Variance and Correlation.** The frontier for the first period (1948-19572) is given by the solid line and the frontier for the last period (1986-2010) is given by the dash-dot line. The dash line and the dotted line represent counterfactual frontiers. The solid line and the dotted line are computed using the same vector of sectoral growth rate and the same sectoral variance. The distance between the solid line and the dotted line shows the effect of the change in the correlation across sectors. The dotted line and the dash line are computed using the same vector of sectoral growth rate and the same correlation across sectors. The distance between the dotted line and the dash line shows the effect of a change in the variance. The dash line and the dash-dot line are computed using the same covariance matrix. The distance between the dash line and the dash-dot line shows the effect of a change in the growth rate. A lower sectoral growth and a higher sectoral variance account for 2/3 and 1/3 of the shift in the frontier, respectively.

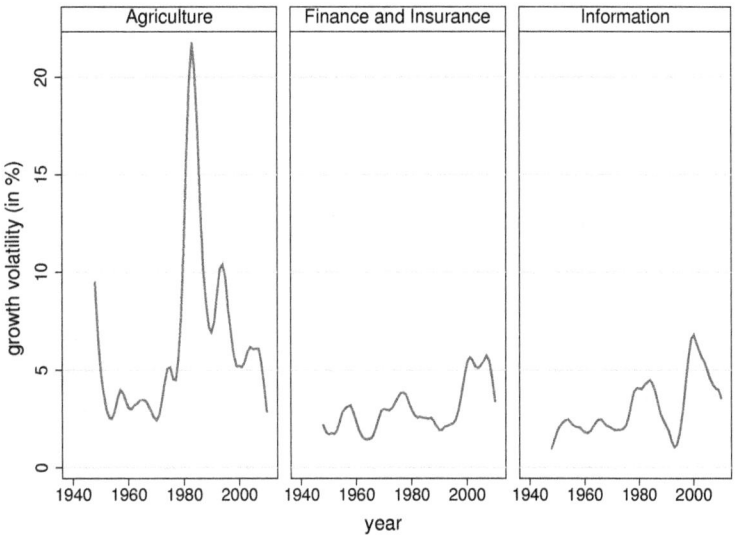

Figure 7: **Sectoral Growth Volatility**. The figure plots the growth volatility for the sectors that have a statistically significant break in volatility.

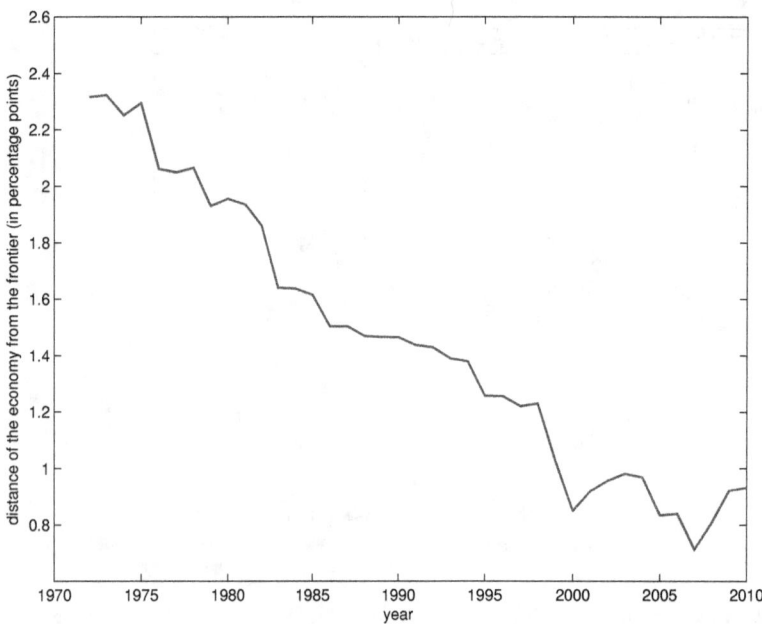

Figure 8: **Distance of the Economy from the Frontier**. The efficiency is measured by the distance of the economy from the frontier. The distance of the economy from the frontier is measured as the minimum distance from each of the portfolios from on the frontier, where the distance is measured in the (growth, volatility) space: $min[D_{i,t}]$, where $D_{i,t} = [(g_{frontier,i,t}-g_{GDP,t})^2+(\sigma_{frontier,i,t}-\sigma_{GDP,t})^2]^{1/2}$. The closer the economy to the frontier the higher the efficiency. A change in the efficiency over time is interpreted as the expected increase in GDP growth, or decline in GDP volatility. For example, the efficiency between 1986-2010 and 1948-1972 increase by 1.39 (the distance of the economy from the frontier was 0.93 in 1986-2010 and 2.32 in 1948-1972). Interpreted along the volatility dimension, if there were no change in the covariance matrix, the GDP volatility in the period 1986-2010 would be 1.39 percentage points lower than in the period 1948-1972.

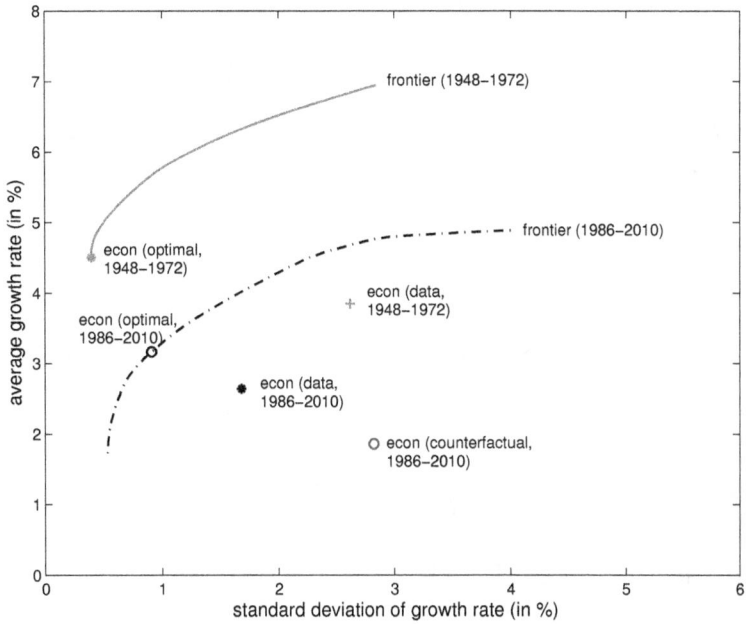

Figure 9: **Efficiency and the Decline in Growth Volatility.** The efficiency of the economy is measured by the distance of the economy from the optimal allocation on the frontier. The distance of the economy from the frontier is given by the distance between the econ(data) and econ(optimal), where econ(optimal) is the optimal allocation on the frontier. As the economy likes GDP growth and dislikes GDP growth volatility, the optimal allocation is determined by the portfolio on the frontier closest to the corresponding econ(data), where the distance is measured in the (growth, volatility) space. The distance of the economy from the frontier has decreased, implying that the efficiency has increased. To illustrated the effect of the increased efficiency in the decline of GDP volatility, I compute a counterfactual economy: econ(counterfactual, 1986-2010) is computed such that the distance of econ(counterfactual, 1985-2010) from frontier(1986-2010) is the same as the distance of the economy from the frontier (1948-1972). If there were no changes in efficiency, there would be no decline in the growth volatility: the GDP volatility in the period 1986-2010, would be 2.82%, which is almost the same as the volatility during the period 1948-1972.

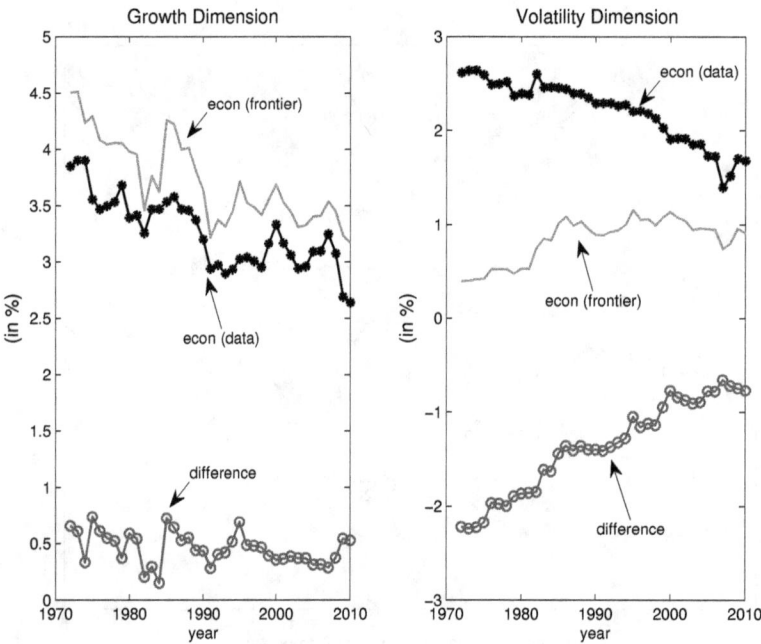

Figure 10: **Risk Efficiency.** This figure plots the improvements in efficiency along the growth and volatility dimension. The distance of the economy from the frontier has been decreasing along the volatility dimension, implying an improvement in the risk efficiency. Efficiency is measured by the distance of the economy from the frontier in the (growth, volatility) space. The optimal allocation is defined as the allocation on frontier closest to the economy.

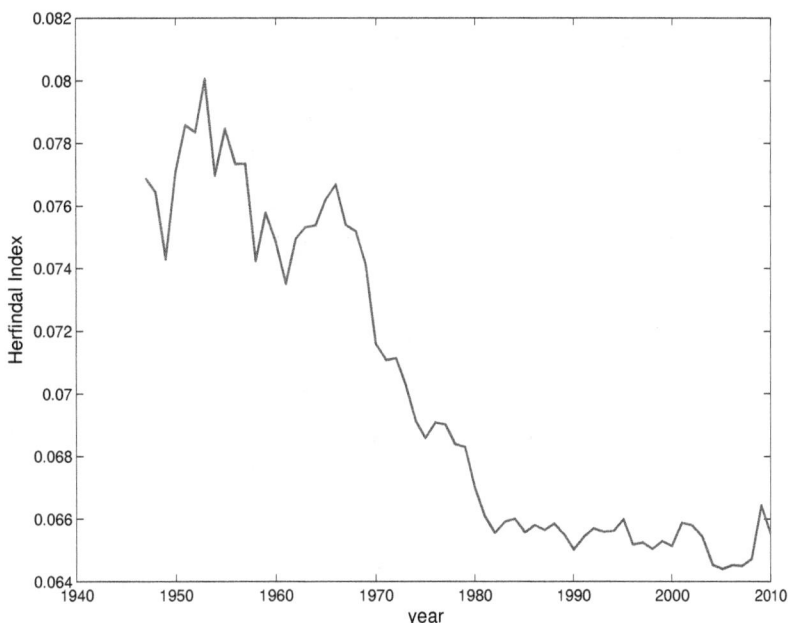

Figure 11: Sectoral Concentration in the Economy. The sectoral concentration is measured by the Herfindal Index, as $\sum \omega_i^2$, where ω_i is the sector share to GDP. The Herfindal Index is calculated using the annual data for 22 broad sectors in the economy. The list of sectors is given in Table 1. The index takes values from 1/n (equal sectoral shares) to 1 (a single sector economy), where n=number of sectors. A decrease in the Herfindal Index corresponds to an increased in diversification. The economy was more diversified during the Great Moderation.

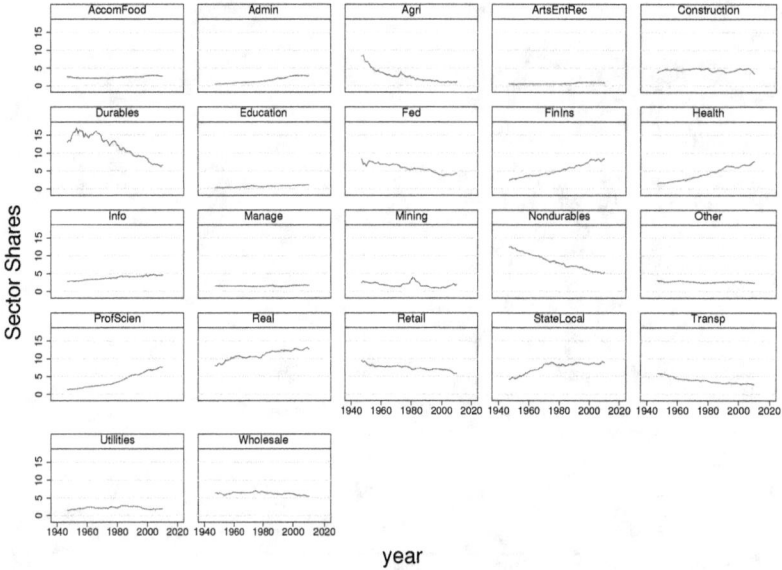

Figure 12: **Sector Shares.** The economy has been shifting away from Agriculture and Manufacturing and moving toward services.

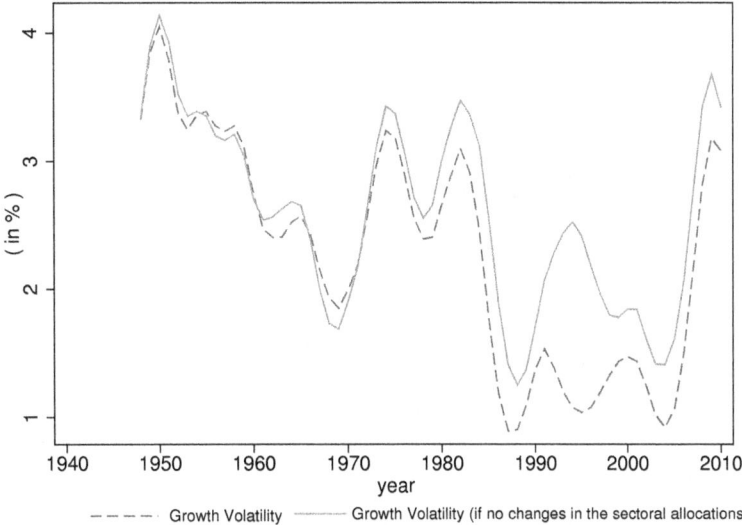

Figure 13: **Sectoral Allocation and GDP Volatility.** The dashed line plots the GDP growth volatility in the data. The solid line plots the growth volatility of a counterfactual GDP series, where the sectoral allocations are time invariant, and the sectoral growth rates vary as in the data. I cannot reject the hypothesis of no break in the counterfactual GDP growth series, providing further support that the decline in GDP growth volatility was the outcome of changes in the sectoral allocations.

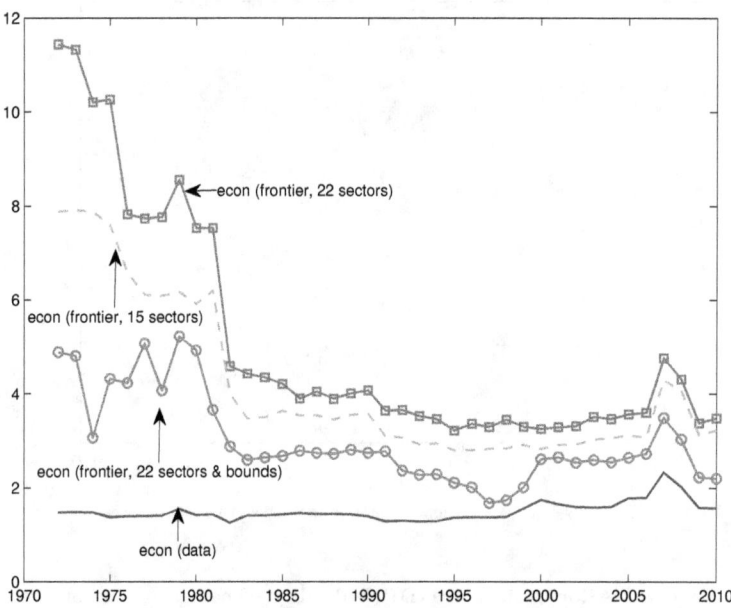

Figure 14: **Preferences: Growth-to-Volatility Ratio.** It is assumed that the economy likes growth and dislikes volatility. The optimal allocation is defined as the allocation on the frontier that minimizes the distance of the economy from the frontier. Growth-to-Volatility Ratio produced by these allocations shows the same pattern across the three specifications. The ratio is lower and stable during the Great Moderation. It takes values from 2 to 4, which is also the range usually used for the coefficient of risk aversion in the the mean-variance utility function.

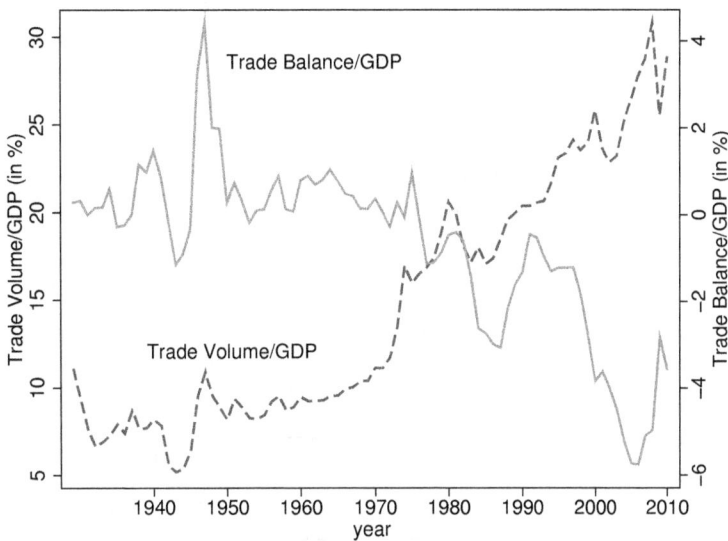

Figure 15: **Trade Balance and Trade Deficit.** The trade volume has been increasing since the 1950s. Trade deficits have been persistent during the Great Moderation.

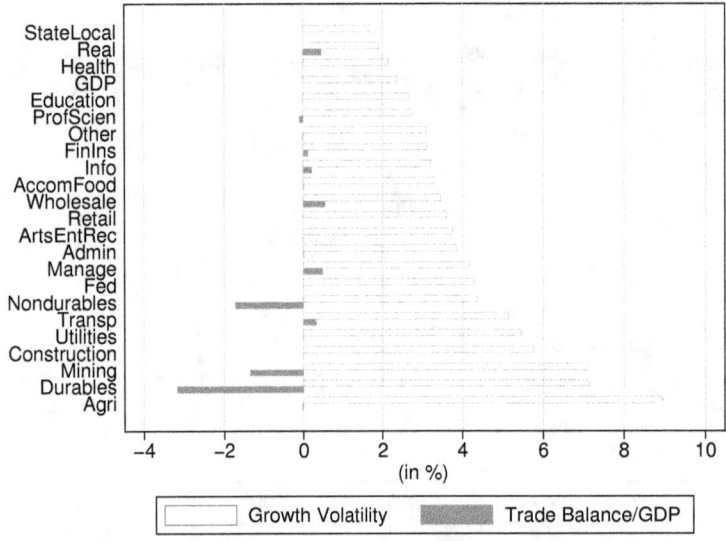

Figure 16: **Growth Volatility and Trade Balance.** The more volatile sectors have a larger trade deficit. The trade data are from the 1998-2009 from the Input-Output Use Tables.

www.ingramcontent.com/pod-product-compliance
Lightning Source LLC
Chambersburg PA
CBHW081805170526
45167CB00008B/3341